Days of the We

Applique Clothing
Designs

Embroidery
Designs

MONDAY

TUESDAY

WEDNESDAY

Days of the Week

Embroidery Designs

Applique Clothing Designs

THURSDAY

FRIDAY

SATURDAY

Days of the Week

Applique Clothing Designs

Embroidery Designs

Iron-On
Cut out each design before using.

SUNDAY

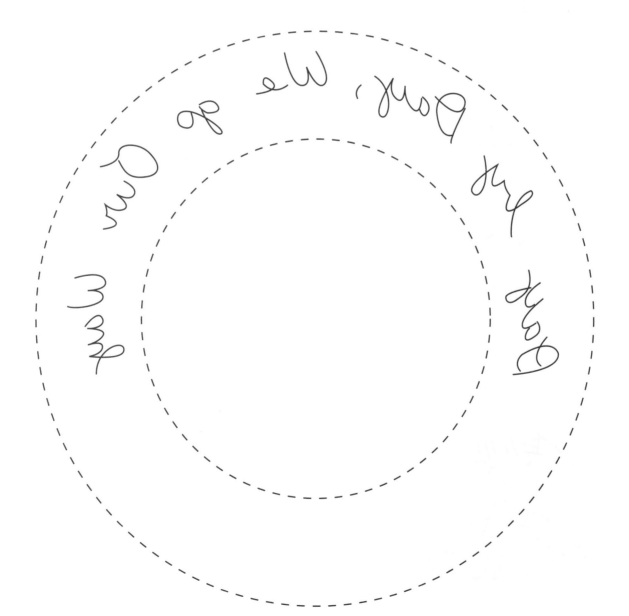

Dark and Dreary Day, We go Our way

Days of the Week

Appliqué Clothing
Designs

Embroider
Designs

iron-On

Cut out each
design before
using

Days of the Week

Appliqué Clothing
Designs

Embroider

Paper Dolls

Embroidery
Designs

Applique Clothing
Designs

Embroidery
Designs

Applique Clothing
Designs

Paper Dolls

Applique Clothing
Designs

Embroidery
Designs

PaperDolls

Appliqué Clothing
Designs

Embroidery
Designs

Appliqué Clothing
Designs

Embroidery
Designs

Paper Dolls

Embroidery Designs

Applique Clothing Designs

Paper Dolls

Applique Clothing Designs

Embroidery Designs

Iron-On
Cut out each design before using.

PaperDolls

Embroidery
Designs

Applique Clothing
Designs

'B' is for Bear

Embroidery
Designs

Appliqué Clothing
Designs

'B' is for Bear

Embroidery

Appliqué Clothing
Designs

'B' is for Bear

Embroidery Designs

Applique Clothing Designs

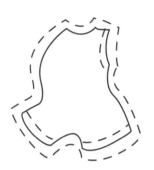

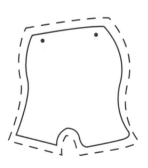

'B' is for Bear

Applique Clothing Designs

Embroidery Designs

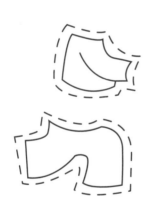

'B' is for Bear

Embroidery
Designs

Applique Clothing
Designs

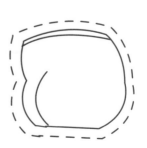

'B' is for Bear

Iron-On
Cut out each design before using.

Applique Clothing Designs

Embroidery Designs

so 'B' is for 'Bear'

...to transfer words - trace from the wrong
...side so they will read right on the quilt

L=lion   P=pig   Z=zebra

F=frog   G=giraffe   H=horse

A=ape   B=bear   B=bunny

'B' is for Bear

To transfer words - trace from the wrong side so they will 'read right' on the quilt.

Z = zebra   P = pig   L = lion

F = frog   H = giraffe   G = horse   F = frog

A = ape   B = bunny   B = bear   A = ape

C = cat   D = dog   E = elephant   C = cat

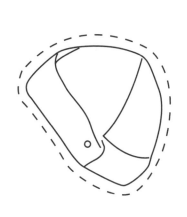

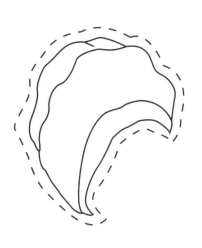

Sugar & Spice

Iron-On
Cut out each design before using.

Applique Clothing Designs

Embroidery Designs

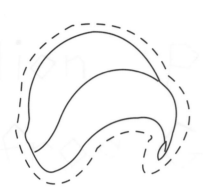

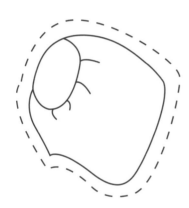
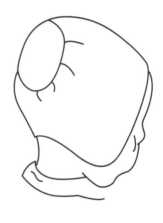

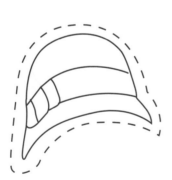

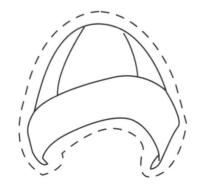

Iron-On
Cut out each
design before
using.

Appliqué Clothing
Designs

Embroidery
Designs

Sugar & Spice

Embroidery Designs

Applique Clothing Designs

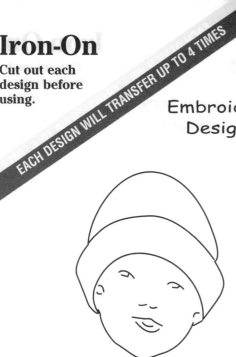
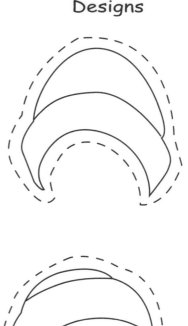

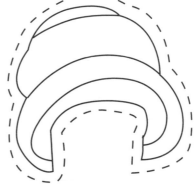

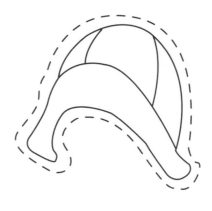

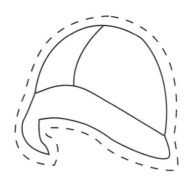

Sugar & Spice

Applique Clothing Designs

Embroidery Designs

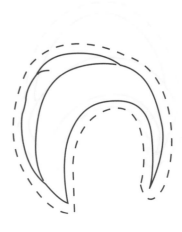

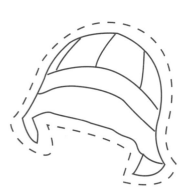

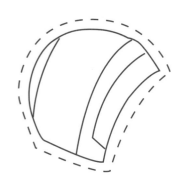

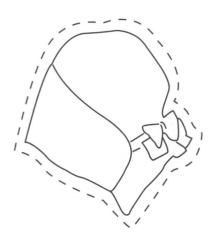

To transfer words - trace from the wrong side
so they will 'read right' on the quilt.